Who I Am

By Michelle Owusu-Hemeng

This book is dedicated to
African-American children everywhere.
You all are wonderfully and beautifully
made. #BlackGirlMagic

Look in the mirror and who do you see?

Do you see the sparkle in your eyes? Do you see the vision of success that is in store for your future?

Do you see your rosy, thick nose with a round poke to it? The nose that allows you to smell all life has to offer.

What about your mouth? Can I see your smile? The way you use those 26 muscles to show off that smile means a lot.

So never let anyone take the joy your smile brings.

Do you see your ears? Have you heard that you are beautiful and smart? You are, and I will repeat it to you forever.

Do you see your beautiful hair? Every kink and every curl is naturally and wonderfully formed.
Embrace it! Love it! Become it!

Do you see your family and friends? Do you see what makes us all unique? We are all different and that is the beauty of it all.

Look in the mirror! Who do you see? I see YOU!!! That person you see looking back at you can be the next president, doctor, nurse, teacher, artist, scientist or whatever you want to be.
Your dreams will become your reality.

Daily Reminders

I love the skin I am in.

I am loved.

I am black and beautiful.

My voice is powerful.

About the Author

Michelle Owusu-Hemeng was born in Fort Worth, Texas and raised in Arlington, Texas. She is the youngest of three. When she is not teaching; she spends her time volunteering at the local orphanage.

She is an advocate for social justice, quality early care and education, where she focuses on creating awareness, building support, working for change, developing professionalism, promoting child and family issues, and informing public policy.